UNIVERSITY OF MINNESOTA

Marianne Moore

BY JEAN GARRIGUE

UNIVERSITY OF MINNESOTA PRESS · MINNEAPOLIS

Printed in the United States of America at
the North Central Publishing Company, St. Paul

Library of Congress Catalog Card Number: 65-64770

Distributed to high schools in the United States by Webster Division
McGraw-Hill Book Company
St. Louis   New York   San Francisco   Dallas

PUBLISHED IN GREAT BRITAIN, INDIA, AND PAKISTAN BY THE OXFORD
UNIVERSITY PRESS, LONDON, BOMBAY, AND KARACHI, AND IN CANADA
BY THE COPP CLARK PUBLISHING CO. LIMITED, TORONTO

MARIANNE MOORE

JEAN GARRIGUE, the poet, has published a number of collections of her work, including *Country without Maps, A Waterwalk by the Villa d'Este, The Monument Rose,* and *The Ego and the Centaur.* She has taught at several colleges and universities.

⤙ *Marianne Moore*

W E K N O W this poet by her voice, by her "astonishing invention in a single mode," by her delicate, taxing technique; we know her for the "relentless accuracy" of her eye.

This is Marianne Moore, ironist, moralist, fantasist.

She was born in 1887 in St. Louis, Missouri, and has written of herself that she is a Presbyterian and was brought up in the home of her grandfather, the Reverend John R. Warner, who was for twenty-seven years the pastor of Kirkwood Presbyterian Church in St. Louis, that her brother was a chaplain in the Navy for forty and more years, and that the books to which she has had access have been, on the whole, serious.

Of her father, John Milton Moore, she has told us little. It is known that he left his family when his daughter was an infant. To her mother, Mary Warner Moore, she paid significant tribute in a postscript to the *Selected Poems*: "In my immediate family there is one 'who thinks in a particular way;' and I should like to add that where there is an effect of thought or pith in these pages, the thinking and often the actual phrases are hers."

In 1894 the family moved to Carlisle, Pennsylvania. It was at Metzger Institute in that town that she was educated and at Bryn Mawr, from which she graduated in 1909. The next year she studied at the Carlisle Commercial College and from 1911 to 1915 was in charge of the commercial department of the United States Indian School at Carlisle. If it remains a curiosity that she taught such subjects as typing and bookkeeping to young Indians it is less surprising, in view of her late pronounced interest in baseball and her early flair for tennis playing, that she coached the boys in field sports. In 1911 she spent a summer in England and France where, in Paris, she went to every museum but two. In 1918 she moved to New York, living on St. Luke's Place, teaching first at a private school. From 1921 to 1925 she was an assistant at the Hudson Park branch of the New York Public Library. Some critics have made something of this (part-time) library work, suggesting that her years of easy accessibility to so many card catalogues and pamphlets gave her the clue to her unique method of happening on a poem. But from Miss Moore's account she was more engaged in reviewing "silent-movie fiction" than in working behind the stacks with well-wormed collections of odd learning, and it would seem that her bent for collecting rare data and, taking "a wing here" and "a leg there," fitting something of them into poems was sufficiently native to her without the experience at the neighborhood library.

Her verse first appeared in *The Egoist*, an English periodical, in *Poetry*, and in Alfred Kreymborg's *Others* in 1915, and later she began to attend those small gatherings held at Kreymborg's apartment in Greenwich Village for such young experimenting poets as Wallace Stevens and William Carlos Williams. Although H. D. had been her classmate at Bryn Mawr, neither knew of the other's "interest in writing"; but in 1921 it was H. D. and Bryher (Winifred Ellerman, then Mrs. Robert McAlmon) who published through the Egoist Press, without the author's knowledge, *Poems*, a collection of 24 that had appeared in English and American magazines.

Ezra Pound had already spoken of her work and Mina Loy's as a kind of "dance of the intelligence" (*logopoeia*) and possessed of an "arid clarity" (*Little Review*, 1918) and in 1923 when a pamphlet of her poems, *Marriage*, was published in the United States and in England, T. S. Eliot wrote: "I can only think of five contemporary poets — English, Irish, French and German — whose works excite me as much or more than Miss Moore's."

By 1920 she was beginning to publish in the *Dial*, that aristo-crat of the vanguards, and in 1925 she received the *Dial* award for "distinguished service to American letters" for *Observations*, her first book to be published in this country. In the same year she be-came acting editor of the *Dial* and remained with it until 1929 when it expired. *Selected Poems* appeared in 1935 with an Intro-duction by Eliot, famous for its pronunciamento: "My conviction, for what it is worth, has remained unchanged for the last fourteen years: that Miss Moore's poems form part of the small body of durable poetry written in our time."

Miss Moore has been brilliantly served from the beginning by the most astute of critics and the most perceptive of poets. If Pound and Eliot took up her cause, a poet-critic like Yvor Winters fur-thered it, and it remains for R. P. Blackmur and Morton Dauwen Zabel to have compounded penetrating estimates of her work. Of a later generation, Randall Jarrell, Lloyd Frankenberg, and Vi-vienne Koch have been brilliant and dedicated. She has not suf-fered from neglect or misunderstanding, and though her work went against the main current and tradition of (English) poetry, she was not scouted for it. Can we say that she was fortunate in being with the *Zeitgeist* rather than against it, or out of it? She has been compared with Emily Dickinson more than once and is it a proof of "progress" or was it a mere lucky accident that she was not penalized for her magnificent originality as Emily was?

In the fifties Miss Moore received from officialdom the recog-nition that poets, critics, and readers had given her for many years, her *Collected Poems* (1951) receiving the Bollingen and Pulitzer prizes and the National Book Award. In 1954 that long labor, her translation of the *Fables* of La Fontaine, appeared and in 1955 *Predilections*, a collection of her reviews and essays. She became a member of the National Institute of Arts and Letters in 1947 and of the American Academy in 1955.

"But we prove, we do not explain our birth," she wrote in "The Monkey Puzzle," and if this does not apply as sharply to life itself nevertheless let the poems lead the way.

Like William Carlos Williams she wanted, when young, to be a painter. But then she also thought of studying medicine and found the biology courses exhilarating. "Precision, economy of statement, logic employed to ends that are disinterested, drawing and identifying, liberate — at least have some bearing on — the imagination, it seems to me," she has said in an interview with Donald Hall in the *Paris Review*. We think we can see the bearing it has had. Might we not attribute to her what she did to Henry James: "a rapture of observation"? For who has held up to inspection more "skeined stained veined variety"? But this fascination with every shade and tone of the "minute particulars" was only one element of many in *Observations*.

Of *Observations* (1924) one might say: it is first and last a voice. The voice of sparkling talk and sometimes very lofty talk, glittering with authority. It has dismissed poetic diction, indeed is rigorous in its exclusion of the traditional or the romantic sensuous word, phrase, and implication. It works in a new area of language and meanings because it has new insights to bring to subjects not before then quite approximated by poetry. It is experimental and/or revolutionary because it is excluding the magical, the lyrical, the incantatory, and the musical; nature and the seasons, the moon, old Floridas of the imagination, the street scene and the fire sale. Bringing a new diction to another kind of "subject matter," it employed the cadences of prose in a rhythm based on speech. But whose speech? If at moments one might think of Congreve, at others of Henry James, it is essentially her uniquely mother-English own, running with a rapid, finely nerved energy. Held tautly to the line articulation, when so finely intermeshed, is meant, like a dance, to last just so long and not a second longer.

8

There are highly visual poems such as "The Fish," "A Grave"; there are epigrammatic poems out to discriminate, not describe; there is "Roses Only," a model of ambiguity, where a virtue is made of writing on two subjects as if they were one and of saying one thing while meaning another. (But this is true of many poems.)

The contours of these poems are sharp and fine-edged — Blake's "hard and wiry lines of rectitude" — like many of the objects described: "the pierced iron shadows of the cedars," "sculptured scimitars." Her liking for the "strict proportions" of the hard and definite equals her care for symmetries of pattern and such mathematical niceties as in "The Fish" where the number of syllables per line in each stanza is 1/3/8/1/6/9 and where the portioning out of syllables works for a fine pointing up by sound, sight, and meaning. That is, the word weights are so balanced and nicely adjusted that (typographically aiding, too, the deaf) the force has to fall where it does, on the telling when not the killing word — i.e., the word that drives all the point of the poem home to the heart. We hear it in

the chasm side is

     dead.

Sound also tends to the crisp and quick, energetic consonants rather than lolling alliterations: "Bundles of lances all alike, partly hid by emeralds from Persia," or "Greece with its goat and its gourds."

With a concern to narrow limits, to reduce the means of expression to what is indispensable, she understands, like certain painters, the necessity of not going beyond the line. Thus the firmness of the contours, the self-containment of the poem, which often goes by a crooked mile to its usually ringing, often epigrammatic close.

If many of the essential characteristics of her style meet the little laws laid down by the Imagists — the absence of introspective self, the concentration upon the object-subject, conciseness, a rhythm "which corresponds exactly to the emotion or shade of emotion" — can we say that Imagism was her distant parent? There are the early brief "To a Chameleon," "An Egyptian Pulled Glass Bottle in the Shape of a Fish," "A Talisman." Like most Imagist poems they are static, concentrated on rendering the one instant of the object as clearly and firmly as possible. But "A Talisman" (1912), selected by Eliot as being the only poem to suggest a slight influence of H. D., rhymes and is formally developed, unlike most Imagist poems, and is conventional beside "To a Chameleon" which is already more free and idiosyncratic and already (1916) taking the syllable as the measure rather than the foot, indicating that if she had learned from the Imagists how to approach the object with an intense scrutiny she had learned almost as soon how to take over a method for strictly her own purposes.

And if *precision* had become the watchword of the Imagists — T. E. Hulme, first Imagist and "father" of them all, is said to have introduced the word to modern literary criticism in his essay "Romanticism and Classicism" and it is known that Pound as early as 1912 was calling for poetry to be as precise as prose — these poems had it, and not only of the "minute discriminations" (Blake) but of the very articulation of movement.

Precision in this case also goes with wit and certain moral and intellectual convictions. Hers is no poetry of emotional conflict or discord or disillusionment either. If in "Bowls" we have an implicit-explicit criticism of the blind worship of the present and in other poems satiric rejections of popular prejudices ("The vestibule to experience is not to / be exalted into epic grandeur"), there is little notice, head-on, of the disorders of the present. The open social scene was not her province. We do not have the flavors of the age in terms of rancid butter or oyster shells. (Her objectified world is in this sense interior.) Two lines in "New York" might sound a theme: "one must stand outside and laugh/since to go in is to be lost." If these lines suggest that laughter can be a weapon of self-preservation, do they not also suggest a recognition of differences about which nothing can be done? It is essential not to go in and be lost.

But in the decade of *The Waste Land* she partakes of no cynical or despairing view. From the first her highly defined world seems based on a clear-cut recognition of ethical values she considers still extant though many would have it proved that such values have been vitally assailed if not destroyed. It might be said that this poet, devoted to the paradox, strikes one as a figure of paradox too: with her clear moral and intellectual convictions not just exactly of the times, but with her forged weapons of technique the pure exemplar of the modernist. But what is a satirist (when she is) who doesn't have strong moral convictions? One is tempted to add that in her case morality seems a facet of sensibility.

One could remark also of her philosophic calm, that strong sense of being in touch with the *adagia*, with a resolute sense of wisdom about life, that it is what has been remarked of the Chinese, "a necessary armor to protect the excessive susceptibility to emotion."

Thus *Observations* brought to verse a new subject matter and to the line a new rhythm, the rhythm of prose in all its succinctness, by this latter completing the circle Flaubert had begun in 1855 when he wrote (in a letter) that he wished to bring the rhythms of poetry to prose. If this book has been equaled by her later books it has never been surpassed and exists a twentieth-century monument like *Harmonium*, *A Draft of XXX Cantos*, and *The Waste Land*.

Like Williams and Cummings she suspected the comma (Apollinaire was the first to do so) and thought it "wholesome" not to capitalize the beginning of lines, disliked the connective (but so did Emily Dickinson) in the interests of intensity. "Titles are chaff," she said in an early poem and circumvented the plague of having to title poems by making the first line serve as title. To such an instance of inventiveness can be added others: notes — listed at the back of each book — and, in the case of *Observations*, even an index appended!

If the notes can't be considered as what's left over of what couldn't be put into the poem, neither can they be considered as necessary for the deeper understanding of the poem. They frequently give us delightful information on, say, the price of unicorn horns, but primarily they serve as a reading list, giving us the authors of those phrases that as specimens of wit have been rescued for us. In this way Miss Moore is a kind of curator of verities and "briefs, abstracts and chronicles" of past literatures. "Acknowledgments seem only honest," said Miss Moore.

This inlaying of quotations with the black hooks that so nicely help to set a brilliance apart has been compared with the collage technique of Braque, Picasso, and Kurt Schwitters. Miss Moore first introduced it in 1915. And her innovation has since become a part of literary tradition.

Her approach to rhyme was also radical. In about half of the poems in *Observations* she avoids it altogether. In "The Fish," "Black Earth," "To Statecraft Embalmed," to name a few, the pattern is formal and the rhyme scheme elaborate. It is rarely insistent, however. Most of the time the rhyme endings are all but submarine in effect because the meaning of the line runs on to the next line and no pause is wanted by the reader, or are so light in sound and echoed so faintly — "Ming" and "something" — that they're almost not heard. (It might be noted that Hopkins wanted his verses to be recited as running on without pause, the rhymes occurring in their midst like a phonetic accident — which is what Miss Moore wanted and got.)

Also wanting a distribution of emphasis more light and even, as in French, she took the syllable as the measure rather than the foot, working always for the effect of unstressed or only faint and lightly stressed rhythms. This was, more or less, an extension of the prose effect. (In three poems puns are suggested on "feet" and we know that in 1918 Miss Moore wrote an article on the unaccented syllable in *The Egoist*. She also wrote in *The Oxford Anthology of American Literature*, Volume II: "Regarding the stanza as a unit, rather than the line, I sometimes divide a word at the end of a line, relying on a general straightforwardness of treatment to counteract the mannered effect.")

Almost from the beginning she proceeds by an express method of her own dialectic. The absurd will rest side by side with the exotic, the commonplace by the exquisite. "There is no progress without contrairies," said Blake and many of her poems seem to have their source in this dictum. They seem to move by the pull of contrasts and by that tension set up. The incongruities and the discrepancies, the contradictions and oppositions — these are what she harnesses and keeps either in tandem or under one yoke.

Juxtaposition of incongruities is of the essence. But not in the ways of other modernists. She is not working with a sensuous language for violently mysterious effects, or juxtaposing words for the sake of shocks of collision. Rather, her language is strictly tempered and clear, almost classical in its moderation and lack of rhetorical splurge. Verb is firmly connected to noun, there is no straining of language within the sentence unit for a tremor of associations setting up strange trains of disrelations. But she did put these clear lines together in such a way that the firm orderly thought or epigram-like description is set next to another in a manner not to have been foreseen. The surprise, the shock, exists in between the spaces that have been leaped over by a swift imagination. Transitions thus seem more like transpositions, a strange flowering of truth upon fact.

If the drama of many a poem lies in the strife of its particulars, we have the same acting against and reacting in the pull of the learned or scientific word against the idiomatic or concrete word: "the elephants with their fog-colored skin/and strictly practical appendages," for example, where "fog-colored" works against the mockery of the abstract words applied to the simple trunk. And words like "occipital" and "phenomena" or such phrases as "cycloid inclusiveness," "fractional magnificence," "hairy carnivora," and "staple ingredients" frequently serve ironic purposes. Then there is the august decorum of "he superintended the demolition of his image in the water by the wind," and "the pulse of its once vivid sovereignty," whose magnificence of phrasing has something of the strange beauty of that poet of the sentence, Sir Thomas Browne. This Latinate-laconic imperious elegance is to be found less in later books. But formal balances and syntactical parallelisms persist. "He is swifter than a horse; he has a foot hard/as a hoof; the leopard/is not more suspicious" (reminding us of Habakkuk) or "the/king gave his name to them and he was named/for them."

In "Injudicious Gardening" (the title itself a small joke) it's as if this poet mocks herself, turning against the musical inflections of the first stanza with the slightly freezing abstractness of the second:

> If yellow betokens infidelity,
>   I am an infidel,
>   I could not bear a yellow rose ill will
>   Because books said that yellow boded ill,
>   White promised well;
>
> However, your particular possession —
>   The sense of privacy
>   In what you did — deflects from your estate
>   Offending eyes, and will not tolerate
>   Effrontery.

14

The colder movement of the Latinate words drawn up to their full height and marched out to rebuke is felt in "Roses Only." Its effect of hectoring hauteur is dependent in part on the formal propriety of its diction and an elaborate sentence structure in which clause succeeds clause with all but martial progress to achieve the permanent brilliance of

> Guarding the
> infinitesimal pieces of your mind, compelling
> audience to
> the remark that it is better to be forgotten than to
> be remembered too violently,
> your thorns are the best part of you.

Both early and late Miss Moore has been a curator of that sacred cow, the statistic. In "Virginia Britannia" the hedge-sparrow "wakes up seven minutes sooner than the lark"; Lapland reindeer in "Rigorists" "run eleven miles in fifty minutes." But it is only in "New York" that the use of a business barbarism — "estimated in raw meat and berries, we could feed the universe" — crisply points up the grand uselessness of such an estimate. In this mimicking of the language of business and other clichés she escapes being flat by being so succinctly sharp. To say it another way, she was one of the first of the poets to take rather intractable antipoetic material, the business phrase, the statistic, the cliché, and by her arrangement of it in relation to other phrases, bend it to her own purposes — i.e., the poetry of the unpoetic. An example is her use of the banking phrase in "Roses Only": "You do not seem to realize that beauty is a liability rather than/an asset." The competency of that has entered the tone of many a poet.

"Marriage," that exercise in paradox, that divertimento of speculation on the "interesting impossibility," is a particularly striking example of the swift transition and the alternating between contraries. William Carlos Williams called it "an anthology of transits." One could also call it a tour de force of digressions, a master-piece of sudden departures. Plying between homage paid to and mockery made of "This institution,/perhaps one should say enter-prise," we see that if it is the public nature of it that arouses deft skepticism it is its private significance that is given such tribute as "This fire-gilt steel/alive with goldenness." But since marriage is both eminently private and public, she can be but in the position of taking away with one hand what she gives with the other. To the subject of love itself — not specifically amorous love but "'the illusion of a fire/effectual to extinguish fire'" which makes mar-riage seem "'a very trivial object indeed'"—she brings nothing less than splendor in two passages, in one of which she puts Adam and Eve into an Eden that has all the quaintness of a primitive woodcut. "Plagued by the nightingale . . . dazzled by the ap-ple." But nothing in this poem stands still. It is premised on the necessity of swiftness and we are no sooner in Eden than out of it, in some drawing room with the "shed snakeskin of politeness," just as we are never far from such sharp turnings of the tables as "'For love/that will gaze an eagle blind . . . from forty-five to seventy/is the best age.'" Its method of progression is not only fleet but abrupt, connectives being dropped or leaped over. Darts are released at women's prejudices against men and men's against women; there are submerged hints of feminist argument at work but these too are tossed off. Guarded, covering up its tracks almost as soon as it makes them, it is a kind of masked dance on the ex-cruciating point of how to be free though in bondage, and at the close we learn that "liberty and union" are perhaps possible only for those with a "simplicity of temper" — if it can be said that the summary is any more important than the *aperçus* dropped along the way.

Does it seem to go by fits and starts? But how many overlappings there are along the way. What matters is the sequence of airy no-tions, what matters is that the wit not be grounded by the heaviness that usually goes with too much expansion. What matters is the impact which the successive words make on us. "Marriage" is a rapidly moving train that once you are on it carries you from glittering landing stage to stage, none of which you are really allowed to get off at, or stay solemnly with. In grasping for analogies, one thinks of Chinese painting which stretches out the viewpoint along the entire panorama so that mountains and waterfalls all appear to be moving toward us, although if such paintings avoid leading the eye into a single depth, this scarcely applies to the poem's action. Word-playing on brilliant surfaces, it alludes as much to depths behind depths. One is tempted to quote Henry James: "To be explicit was to betray divinations."

In "The Past Is the Present" she has not only fallen upon her form early, she is defining for us, although she is speaking about Hebrew poetry, what it is that she is doing and going to be doing. Or so, at least, we can interpret it in view of all the poems that followed. Moreover she announces early (the poem was first printed in *Others* in 1915) one of her touchstones. And this is no less than the Bible. (We see by the notes in *Observations* how many phrases from George Adam Smith's *The Expositor's Bible*, Richard Baxter's *The Saints Everlasting Rest*, A. R. Gordon's *The Poets of the Old Testament*, how many phrases too from ministers' sermons, are inlaid into poems. Is it incidental or not that in a Foreword to the *Marianne Moore Reader* (1961) she should write: "My favorite poem? asked not too aggressively — perhaps recalling that Henry James could not name his 'favorite letter of the alphabet or wave of the sea.' The Book of Job, I have sometimes thought . . .") If we remember that early period when the Imagists had already set verse free and damned rhyme, we can think of this poem as being the last word in an intense argument held in some book-lined room:

If eternal action is effete
  and rhyme is outmoded,
    I shall revert to you
  Habakkuk, as on a recent occasion I was goaded
      into doing by XY, who was speaking of unrhymed
        verse.
This man said — I think that I repeat
  his identical words:
     'Hebrew poetry is
  prose with a sort of heightened consciousness.' Ecstasy
     affords
       the occasion and expediency determines the form.

If external action (plot — in literature? resolution — in life) is effete and *if* rhyme is outmoded (assumptions of the unseen argufier made to seem both absurd and pretentious), if the new broom of the present wants to sweep half the past away, she will revert to Habakkuk. Nothing later than that minor prophet of the Bible, and nothing more fashionable. Is the goading XY the same "this man" who delivers the energizing definition of Hebrew poetry that can and will be applied to her own work? "Prose with a sort of heightened consciousness"? The Reverend Edwin H. Kellogg is credited in the notes with "Hebrew poetry is prose" but to this has been added the very important "with a sort of heightened consciousness." The heightening of consciousness is all and an answer in the argument. There is verse and verse. Bad free verse is simply prose without that heightening. Moreover she herself is using rhyme in this poem, unlike old Habakkuk. And in the last line she kicks away from the contradictions inherent in the situation to hand us with abrupt decisiveness the keys to the secret of the creative instant. "Ecstasy affords the occasion and expediency determines the form." "Expediency" is the shock word here following so close on "ecstasy." You might say that it disinfects a word so much distrusted in this century. (Much later, in "The Hero," we have: "looking/upon a fellow creature's error with the feelings of a mother — a/woman or a cat" where "cat" takes the curse off "mother," let alone "woman.") Nevertheless, ecstasy it is. One does what one can with the lightening flash. How to seize it except by the most expedient method at hand? Form, it would seem, is determined by the raptus. "Spirit creates form" ("Roses Only"). Is form to be equated with the shell that the mollusk makes, his being's expediency too, the artist's form as organic to himself as the shell is to the snail? Miss Moore has defined it for us: "I feel that the form is the outward equivalent of a determining inner conviction, and that the rhythm is the person."

The force and fire of Biblical language is also a subject of "Novices" but before we arrive at it an artillery of wit is brought to bear on a kind of overrefined and underfed modern literary mind "confusing the issue," "blind to the right word, deaf to satire." The poem glitters with so much summed-up intensity that its energy feels like — is it Irish? fury? A fury of byplay, at least. "Acquiring at thirty what at sixty they will be trying to forget . . . they write the sort of thing that would in their judgment interest a lady; / curious to know if we do not adore each letter of the alphabet that goes to make a word of it." The raillery continues: "according to the Act of Congress, the sworn statement of the treasurer and all the rest of it," which is surely calculated to reduce the opponent to a recognition of his own asininity. Other sidewise allusions, metaphorical extensions such as in the lines beginning "Dracontine cockatrices" and those on the "lucid movements of the royal yacht," contribute to the argument more elaborately, the latter lines preparing for the tremendous onslaught of the powerful and dazzling conclusion. And certainly the finical quibblings, the "willowy wit" of those, one suspects, all-too-precious novices, who are bored incidentally by "the stuffy remarks of the Hebrews," get what they deserve as the "unforced passion of the Hebrew language" is hurled at them. What begins in witty ire ends in a grandeur not far from the Miltonic sublime as two authorities meet — the sea and Biblical language:

> Obscured by 'fathomless suggestions of colour',
> by incessantly panting lines of green, white with concussion,
> in this drama of water against rocks — this 'ocean of hurrying
>   consonants'
> with its 'great livid stains like long slabs of green marble',
> its 'flashing lances of perpendicular lightning' and 'molten fires
>   swallowed up',
> 'with foam on its barriers',
> 'crashing itself out in one long hiss of spray'.

The action of language is developed in terms of the action of the waters, and all in a blaze of glory and claps upon claps of energy. The method is to rush you into splendor and leave you with dazzle. "People's Surroundings" ends with such a triumphant progress, "The Monkeys" in a burst almost as breathtaking:

> — strict with tension, malignant
> in its power over us and deeper
>   than the sea when it proffers flattery in exchange for
>   hemp,
> rye, flax, horses, platinum, timber, and fur.

This roll call of nouns in the last line is a choice example of Moorish sound at its finest and it is an effort to remember that they are but shipper's items transmuted into splendor. The unexpected contiguity of flax with horses and timber, so hard a substance, with rich fur — thus this poem that begins with the drolleries of the zoo moves into high comedy when a cat makes a speech worthy of any autocrat defending the art of the few against the Dunciad many. His astringent remarks on those protesting that they can't understand the new and difficult in art (Brancusi, Picasso? — this poem was first published in 1917) has a further refinement of irony, for the cat scorns these objects of his wit for suspecting art to be just what it really is: "strict with tension, malignant in its power over us and deeper than the sea . . ."

"The Labours of Hercules" undergoes a similar mutation, commencing with the absurd and by a series of progressions closing on the note of a moral rhetoric which is to have an echo later in "In Distrust of Merits" and " 'Keeping Their World Large.' " Formally it is a series of propositions couched in the infinitive, "To popularize the mule," etc., and with the same kind of symmetrical nicety closes with another kind of grammatical repetition:

> 'that the Negro is not brutal,
> that the Jew is not greedy,
> that the Oriental is not immoral,
> that the German is not a Hun.'

Shifting after its humorous opening to the literary-critical note, "to teach the bard with too elastic a selectiveness/that one detects creative power by its capacity to conquer one's detachment," it arrives after two extensions or witty divagations at

> to prove to the high priests of caste
> that snobbishness is a stupidity,
> the best side out, of age-old toadyism,
> kissing the feet of the man above,
> kicking the face of the man below

which in its directness of putting the quality of boot-licking under the most searching light has an effect of almost shockingly savage insight. Beginning with humor, ending with the moral imperative, this poem has, like "The Monkeys" and "Novices," its pattern of progress until, the reversal achieved, we are in another field of thought.

"Those Various Scalpels" not so much progresses as changes key, if one may revert to the musical analogy, and in the phrase "rustling in the storm/of conventional opinion," drives with ruthless swiftness to the heart of the matter: all this wrought artfulness

JEAN GARRIGUE

of appearance, this Renaissance-jewel-encrusted and farthingaled
semblance of the utmost of aristocratic vanity — for what? Nothing
more than *conventional opinion*? We are prepared and not prepared for this swift reversal by the ringing insistence of the repeti-
tions "your hair," "your eyes," "your raised hand" which, for all
the tribute that so much intent attention implies, warn us by their
pain-suggesting images of "eyes, flowers of ice/and/snow sown by
tearing winds on the cordage of disabled ships" and "your cheeks,
those rosettes/of blood on the stone floors of French châteaux"
with its hint of shadowy plots and sudden assassinations. That
this epitome of sterile cruelty whose arrows are lances (nicely hid
by jewels), whose weapons are surgical instruments, that this idol
of a frigid self-involvement whose beauty can give nothing but
pain, is rebuked with a brilliance surpassing the brilliances that
described her is a spectacular achievement:

                                        But
why dissect destiny with instruments which
   are more highly specialized than the tissues of destiny itself?

Otherwise one sees in this poem how the visual is tempered by
the abstract, how repetition of phrasal structure is employed for
an imposing rhetorical effect, how the symmetrical stanzas (two of
nine lines and three of eight lines) have in each stanza a one-
syllable first line, a last line of four, three, or two syllables, a third
line usually of twelve or fourteen syllables, and how the whole
effect of shape, of repetition, emphasizes the formal splendor of
the phrasing. The effect makes for a sense of volume, of receding
planes and sudden perspectives as in architecture, or in baroque
music.

Miss Moore created a new form (to fit her manner) primarily
by means of a new rhythm, a new way of organizing details and
the insights that spring from them. But there is no critical termi-
nology for this new form and one has to fall back on old ways of

22

classifying. Call "A Grave" a soliloquy if you like, and "New York" too. Or call "Roses Only," that lecture to a flower who is also, it would seem, a woman, a kind of version of the moral essay. Call "People's Surroundings," that study of the kind of places people make for themselves, and "Sea Unicorns and Land Unicorns," that fanciful treatise on the power of the mind to make immoderate legends and to reason almost anything into existence — call them both descriptive essays. But the terms "moral essay" and "descriptive essay" are grab-bag terms and don't really apply. The culmination, in any case, of this kind of free-ranging discursive structure for which there is no term is to be found in "An Octopus," that stupendous aggregate of minerals, animals, weathers, while "Sea Unicorns and Land Unicorns" anticipates the more circuitous organization of Miss Moore's later work. In the latter, her manner with the marvel, the fantastical, is to be methodical, as if giving us information in part. This treatment of the fabulous as if it were quite as probable as the so-called fact wonderfully emphasizes its rare lusters. The poem rises and falls, alternating between passages like " 'cobwebs, and knotts, and mulberries' " and "Britannia's sea unicorn with its rebellious child." In a differing fashion for purposes of humor and for the subtle sake of contrast there will be amidst the rare knowledges and textures the opposing note of " 'in politics, in trade, law, sport, religion' " — a broad sober worldly tone which counteracts the elegant quaintness and faery richness of " 'myrtle rods, and shafts of bay.' " And this dynamics of some high pitch of verbal excitement frequently succeeded by a calm or ironic or dryly prosaic passage is to be found in many poems.

(This poem is also an instance of the way she makes a new unity out of parts of old learnings and culled phrases. In later work, from "The Jerboa" to "Elephants," one sees even more complex examples of this drawing upon all kinds of sources to create a new imaginative reality. In "The Plumet Basilisk" Miss Moore weds the legendary, the naturalistic, and history with a scarcely restrained sumptuousness to present to us the half-miraculous attributes of a very real creature. Chinese legends relate him to the great dragons of the East; myths of "the chieftain with gold body" and the jade, the amethysts, and the pearls of half an Incan empire are gathered in to gild his little gorgeousness. A love of the marvelous is combined with factual notations (obtained from the *Illustrated London News* and other sources) to re-create a beast whose very being seems to be one more proof of Nature's pure fantasy. Has zoology truly such instances? Yes. And in "Nine Nectarines" there is the haunting bit of knowledge on the "red-cheeked peach" that according to ancient Chinese thought "cannot aid the dead,/but eaten in time prevents death." Declared in passing, that knowledge is there to give us the tang, the taste of incredible theory.)

"People's Surroundings" is notably a shuttling between the opposites, a play on that favorite eighteenth-century device, the antithesis, as it tacks here and there, creating rich effects that it contradicts a few lines later, pitting splendors against absurdities, the utilitarian against the artful, movement being one of its powers. Stylistically the poem alternates between the crisp speech rhythms setting forth the plain or efficient and two grand flights, the one beginning with Bluebeard's tower and the closing section which is a very Whitman catalogue, if you will (one line beautifully echoes him: "in magnificent places, clean and decent"), a very cavalry charge, a pure poetry of namings:

> captains of armies, cooks, carpenters,
> cutlers, gamesters, surgeons and armourers,
> lapidaries, silkmen, glovers, fiddlers and ballad-singers

The rich appreciation of the ridiculous in this poem, from the "vast indestructible necropolis" of office furniture to "the municipal bat-roost of mosquito warfare," crops up again in "England" in the greatly gay originality of "plain American which cats and dogs can read!"

And when there is not the satirical that crisps the line, there is its easier twin, humor. If the irony preserves (like amber), the humor sweetens. In later work humor becomes allied with fantasy. In *Observations* it frequently seems a kind of irrepressible outburst — from the fir trees, "austere specimens of our American royal families," to "the spiked hand/that has an affection for one/and proves it to the bone" (though the first is a joke and the latter a pun).

At one or not with this sense of humor is the apt harnessing of the likely with the unlikely, even the "antipoetic." Thus the "industrious" waterfall, the not lulling but plaguing nightingale, young bird voices compared to the intermittent "squeak/of broken carriage-springs," this latter a refreshing accuracy that produces in the reader that nervous response which to some extent resembles what is provoked by the experience itself. Not only has an unhackneyed equivalent been found, but a new association has widened the field of reference, modified it too. For it is the squeak of *carriage-springs*, the something slightly antiquated.

And isn't humor that relishes the incongruity and notices the irrelevancy a facet of candor and honesty, and a part of a desire to see the whole and not to exclude the just incidentally thorny or what cannot be classified, the contradictory? Surely in league with it seems the appreciation for "naturalness" whether it is that of the hippopotamus or Peter the cat or the "mere childish attempt . . . to make a pup/eat his meat from the plate."

This taste for the spontaneous, the "beautiful element of unreason," "a tireless wolf," "a wild horse taking a roll," might be contrasted to the connoisseur's zest for "the hair-seal Persian sheen," old Waterford glass, or for what, when it is rare, could not be more rare, when it is jeweled, the most jeweled, when it is blue, a dragonfly blue. The larger, looser, bolder touch — "The tug . . . dipping and pushing, the bell striking as it comes," and "when the wind is from the east,/the smell is of apples, of hay" — is about as strong an element in her work as these curio-collector notations are.

In nine poems Miss Moore is both poet and critic, writing incidentally about literature in general or poetry in particular. Was she also telling her readers just what it was that she herself had set out to do? Jean-Paul Sartre has said that there is no new technique without a metaphysic. And because her approach to the poem was so radically different, did she have her interests in setting forth as plainly as a subtle mind might her own intentions? One might make a case for this in looking at the celebrated "Poetry" with its shocker of a first line: "I, too, dislike it: there are things that are important beyond all this fiddle." It is an early poem (1919). It is also a difficult poem. Seemingly straightforward, it is oblique when you look into it and complex in terms of what's left out as well as what's put in. And with its iconoclastic and reformist frankness it is upsetting a good many apple carts.

The tone of the opening is cutting. "Reading it, however, with a perfect contempt for it." Why should poetry have to be read with a perfect contempt? And whose poetry? All poetry? Then it turns out that it is not all poetry that is being talked about, that it is possibly just the poetry of her contemporaries — or even not all her contemporaries. It is the poetry of "half poets" and when she dislikes their "fiddle" it is when it is "so derivative as to become unintelligible." What, then, is being argued for? The opposite of the derivative — the original, the honest, the "genuine." A new touchstone is being set up. This touchstone is not the old and famous *beautiful and true*. It is the *genuine*. There is more to be said about the *genuine*. "Hands that can grasp, eyes/that can dilate, hair that can rise,/if it must, these things" — signs of the emotional animal — "are important not because a/high-sounding interpretation can be put upon them but because they are/useful." The *genuine* is, then, the *useful*, the functional. But since there are a great many uses of the word "useful" and we are most acquainted with it in its dreariest, most utilitarian sense, the word has a double edge. *Useful*. Isn't the poet just possibly taunting the aesthetes by choosing a word with such hateful, factual, hard edges? A word that can also be called an epitome of understatement — as if to say the sky is *useful*, or rain, the sun, or for that matter poetry. There is another challenging section. We learn of what is more important than "all this fiddle." It is "the bat/holding on upside down . . . elephants pushing, a wild horse taking a roll . . . the base/ball fan, the statistician . . . and 'business documents and/school-books.' "

A prodigious activity somehow gets set up between these assorted items and by their selection Miss Moore tells us as exactly as analogy can do "what is important." Not only the star, the rose, the sea, but matters and subjects not already made acceptable by literary tradition. "One must make a distinction/however: when dragged into prominence by half poets, the result is not poetry."

A fresh subject matter is not enough. In order to make it seem true poets must be "literalists of the imagination." A poet must imagine so exactly and astutely that, in the words of Morton Dauwen Zabel, he can "see the visible at the focus of intelligence where sight and concept coincide and where it becomes transformed into the pure and total realism of ideas."

Furthermore, without the "imaginary gardens (with real toads in them)" which is a symbol for the aesthetic order, the arrangement of these "phenomena" in a modifying structure and texture, the wolf or the what-not, will only seem "dragged in." It will not have been assimilated, it will acquire no new reality, and it will have lost its original own. There will be no poem, in short. Only a half poem.

(Miss Moore's heightening of the phrase of William Butler Yeats on Blake — "He was a too literal realist of the imagination" — is famous. By portmanteau effect she rendered a daring new meaning. Like many of her finest phrases it combines opposites as compactly as possible. Such paradoxes are her elixirs.)

When this poem appeared in the second edition (1925) of *Observations* it was quite another animal, for it was stripped from its original thirty lines (in *Poems*) to thirteen lines, stripped, too, of its complexities. The bat, et cetera, are still there, but they are "pleasing" rather than "important," and the main emphasis is upon clarity:

> but when they have been fashioned
> into that which is unknowable,
> we are not entertained.
> It may be said for all of us
> that we do not admire what we cannot understand;
> enigmas are not poetry.

In *Selected Poems* it returns to the original version save for the omission of three phrases, and has not been altered since.

If Miss Moore was making a strong stand for intelligibility and clarity in this version of "Poetry" she criticizes the "unknowable" in other poems. "In the Days of Prismatic Colour" there are the lines

> complexity is not a crime but carry
> it to the point of murki-
> ness and nothing is plain

and a variation in "Picking and Choosing":

> Words are constructive
> when they are true; the opaque allusion — the simulated
> flight
> upward — accomplishes nothing.

"When I Buy Pictures" concludes:

> It comes to this: of whatever sort it is,
> it must be 'lit with piercing glances into the life of things';
> it must acknowledge the spiritual forces which have made it.

In other poems there are other critica dicta, all struck off with dashing authority as if on the spur of the moment.

In his Introduction to the *Selected Poems* T. S. Eliot classified the poetry of Marianne Moore as descriptive rather than lyrical or dramatic. But to what new uses description is put! And is such a poem as "New York" simply descriptive? Is it not a turning and unfurling upon a given point: the commercial statistic that New York (in 1921) was the center of the wholesale fur trade? A bizarre enough "fact" in view of all else that the city was the center of — from which the poem leaps straight off into "starred with tepees of ermine and peopled with foxes,/the long guard-hairs waving two inches beyond the body of the pelt." This latter line of a strange half-humorous beauty, a detail (of furrier's knowledge) within a detail, is complemented by an even more rarefied detail on deerskins and these two by the aside, later on, that quotes the follied vanity of a Gonzaga duchess: "'if the fur is not finer than such as one sees others wear,/one would rather be without it.'"

If these extensions of texture (in more ways than one) act as brief rests or pauses, the poem otherwise moves swiftly in a continuousness of visual action which allows for no intrusion of what would thin out its density. Thus by no other transition than the phrase "It is a far cry" we are with "'the queen full of jewels'" and "the beau with the muff" and the contrasting of two pasts with some only implied hint that English palefaces bought furs from redskins at that fur-trading center, the conjunction of the Monongahela and the Allegheny. For this is not the vital point: the vital point is that "scholastic philosophy of the wilderness/to combat which one must stand outside and laugh/since to go in

is to be lost." If the subjective depth of this sets up many questioning echoes, we have at least one answer. "It is not the dime-novel
exterior,/Niagara Falls, the calico horses and the war-canoe." It
is not even "the plunder." It is, in Henry James's phrase, " 'accessibility to experience.' " *Accessibility to experience* — a pre-
scription for the artist! The poem juggles with the past, the
present, Europe, America, outlandish and wonderful Indian
names until the grand light of James's phrase gives one answer,
too, to staying outside. *Accessibility* suggests that one may go in-
side, even be lost, agreeably.

Of these specificities which are not cloyed by generalizations,
one remembers that "to explain is to deform." In this poem of
as much wit as description, passage must be rapid. Another poet
might have lingered with the beauties of deerskins and wilting
eagle's-down in which case the point of the wit might have been
dulled. And if we are with the furs one moment and the " 'queen
full of jewels' " the next, it is up to us to consider the impact of the
contrast between two pasts, both of which are our heritage.

Of the maintenance of such tension Miss Moore has this to say
in an essay called "Feeling and Precision," first published in the
Sewanee Review in 1944: ". . . expanded explanation tends to
spoil the lion's leap — an awkwardness which is surely brought
home to one in conversation . . . Yet the lion's leap would be
mitigated almost to harmlessness if the lion were clawless, so precision is both *impact* and exactitude, as with surgery; and also in
music, the conductor's signal . . . which 'begins far back of the
beat, so that you don't see when the down beat comes. To have
started such a long distance ahead makes it possible to be exact.
Whereas you can't be exact by being restrained.' "

One is exact just because one is so aware of so many shades of
meaning or of "ivory white, snow white, oyster white and six
others." And in the same way that the conductor's beat must begin

far back of the downbeat, the poem acquires its power by virtue of the distance it has to travel before the poet's perceptions can encompass the range of his feeling.

Again, "The Monkey Puzzle" encloses its theme so thickly in arresting particulars that it is tempting to be adrift with them, charmed by the strange freshness, simply content with the out-raying allusions to the Foo dog and Flaubert's Carthage. Its sub-ject is, however, a rare pine tree, "a complicated starkness," a "this [that] is beauty" growing in a fastness and like Gray's desert flower, unseen, unknown, "in which society's not knowing is colossal,/the lion's ferocious chrysanthemum head seeming kind by comparison." The force of this astounding comparison (and the oxymoron that makes the lion a little less fearful but far more beautiful) serves only to intensify the plight of this rare tree that "knows" (trees have prescience, cats talk like artists, elephants philosophize, and jaybirds don't know Greek) " 'it is better to be lonely than unhappy.' " Its isolation as profound as any early American genius's, what can it do but endure its own singularity in its own irreparable solitude? This is to bring perhaps too much to the surface what is implied and embodied in a visual intricacy not unlike the tree's own thicket.

This concreteness can sometimes make a poem seem almost un-possessable on first reading because the meanings are so realized in the specificities themselves. These lines from "The Jerboa" might serve to illustrate: "Those who tended flower/beds and stables were like the king's cane in the/form of a hand." It is for the sake of compression and the desire not to obstruct the move-ment of the poem that the king's attitude toward the poor is per-sonified. But the sting of the observation may not come at once: that the king depends on the poor as he would on a cane, that they are simply commodities to him, to be useful, as a cane is. The visual strangeness of a cane "in the form of a hand" may so divert the reader that he forgets to consider its significance. Sometimes, too, the argument of a poem may be submerged, only to emerge openly, at certain moments. The poem moves in its maze of associations, the disconnected connections magnetized in a manner we cannot see on first acquaintance. And always Miss Moore states but doesn't "explain." Or lines may be of such an epigrammatic rigor that the very parts seem like wholes, or poems within poems. This alone (from "Snakes, Mongooses"), "one is compelled to look at it as at the shadows of the alps/imprisoning in their folds like flies in amber, the rhythms of the skating rink," is but one example of those perceptions compact as definitions, brimming with the energy of having pinned it down and gotten it right. Charles Lamb has spoken of the obscurity of too much meaning. Intense clarity can also blind, like the sun at noon.

But as to all this and as to those poems where the clarity of the image and the density of allusion make for that fascinating combination of what is both lucid and ambiguous at the same time, Miss Moore has, as usual, the last word: "A few unexplained difficult things — they seem to be the life-blood of variety."

As for that "mystery of construction," "An Octopus," though it does not necessarily divert "one from what was originally one's object" (to quote from "England"), it does delay one along the way as description becomes a kind of plot and its own drama. All is in action, from the old glacier itself that "hovers forward 'spider fashion/on its arms'" to its fir trees with "their dark energy of life," its animals, seen in some characteristic behavior and on the move, even its stationary flowers active in their complications of colors and designs.

In its serial construction there is a regular recurrence of outriding phrases that allow for sidelights, tangential glances sometimes pert in tone such as the line on the icy glacier itself, "made of glass that will bend — a much needed invention," or lines that permit us to consider the sheer deadness of **Park Portfolio** language when it is legal or such purely "poetic" extensions (of the ponies with glass eyes) as "brought up on frosty grass and flowers/ and rapid draughts of ice-water." Not to forget the mountain guide in his pleasing "two pairs of trousers." The aside, the brief digression, the Jamesian parenthesis might be called a part of the Moore method and are to be found in many poems. They serve, as they do in "An Octopus," to make for a kind of brio of the irrelevantly relevant and for the effect that R. P. Blackmur phrased so acutely: "husky with unexhausted detail . . . containing inexhaustibly the inexplicable."

In the last section, about the Greeks, which also gives another character to the glacier,

> Relentless accuracy is the nature of this octopus
> with its capacity for fact

(as if it were a terribilita of an artist), one sees how the tempo at which one must read is dictated. The passage begins slightly after "The Greeks liked smoothness"

> ascribing what we clumsily call happiness,
> to 'an accident or a quality,
> a spiritual substance, or the soul itself,
> an act, a disposition, or a habit,
> or a habit infused, to which the soul has been persuaded,
> or something distinct from a habit, a power—'
> such power as Adam had and we are still devoid of.

As if Experience were correcting Theory, this kind of Schoolman's ethereal speculation in finely defining phrase upon phrase, one qualifying the other and all kept in musical suspension, is given this forceful, brusque stop, a stop even to our hopes.

In "Camellia Sabina" there is the same kind of rapid moving out onto a single hard flashing line after the airy humors and mercurial play of the "upland country mouse" dashing around the "*concours hippique*" of the grape-arbor "in a flurry/of eels, scallops, serpents/and other shadows . . . The wine-cellar? No/It accomplishes nothing and makes the/soul heavy" — the abruptness of this and the swift change of rhythm severely preparing us for the renunciatory "The gleaning is more than the vintage."

From the *Selected Poems* (1935) on we see more "inscape," hear more music, meet more fantasy and far more animals. Stanzaic structure is more elaborate together with a new complexity of detail, the line is more musically nuanced, with more verbal interplay and more sub-patterns of internal rhymings and end-rhymings. The ironist and the satirist has been succeeded by the fantasist-humorist, and the hard-driving electrical speed of the free-verse line (as exemplified by the ruthless, relentless progression of a poem like "A Grave") by more light and subtle rhythms. Seven of the eight new poems of *Selected Poems* are seven new departures. One is not like the other. In each a new version of a form is explored. In "The Frigate Pelican" one can fancy that form is in part imitative, so deftly are the rhythms of flight suggested by certain lines and by word-plays; there is a gliding from one stanza to another, like the feints of bird-winging. The thickly woven texture of "The Plumet Basilisk," that essay on dragonhood, is so closely qualified that it suggests the very density of tropical vegetation. Of later poems "Virginia Britannia" (*What Are Years*, 1941) takes description to a new height. As one of her many place poems, it is of flowers, birds, and history so interwoven that its long lines seem to move like feelers, reaching out and advancing on all sides at once, the theme of colonizing arrogance (as symbolized by the strangler figs) growing out of the very elements of the scene and at one with it. In these instances detail is given a new kind of day and with it, necessarily, a slowing of tempo, or delayings and detainings by Hopkins-esque word clusters. Such word clusters do what Hulme in 1915 or so asked the new poetry to do ("to make you continuously see a physical thing, to prevent you from gliding through an abstract process") and aid in compacting multiple parts swiftly for the sake of impact.

The high interest in design and pattern, first seen in "The Fish" (1918), is carried on in "Nine Nectarines" in which precision of sight — even a subdividing of it — is heard in the intricately echoing fineness of sound. And "The Jerboa" with its neatness and firmness achieves an especial kind of visual and aural beauty by virtue of its flexibly confining pattern, the six-line stanza with a rhyme scheme that exerts the nicest control over the faint chimings. Working with highly selected clarities of dapple dog-cats and small eagles, it evolves (in the first section) into a kind of tale-telling, a rigorously simplified recounting of the habits and tastes of a people forgotten save by historians and encyclopods. They are "violently remembered" in this poem:

> Lords and ladies put goose-grease
> paint in round bone boxes with pivoting
> lid incised with the duck-wing

> or reverted duck-
> head

The acuteness of the visual achievement might be exemplified with the power of

> the wild ostrich herd
> with hard feet and bird
> necks rearing back in the
> dust like a serpent preparing to strike,

and delicacy of sound by "They looked on as theirs/impallas and onigers."

The concern to strike for the resonances of color that we see in the "coachwheel yellow" of "Critics and Connoisseurs" — which gives us at least two sensations at once, the pleasure of the coachwheel and the shade of its color — is to be found in "duck-egg

35

greens, and egg-plant blues" (note the nice balancing of consonants) or "calla or petunia/white." Instead of a metaphor we are
given a further qualification. Such precisions both intensify the
experience and keep it under close control as the measurements
and temperatures of what's seen are exactly taken. Her "pride,
like the enchanter's,/is in care, not madness." With the lines

> in the stiff-leafed tree's blue-
> pink dregs-of-wine pyramids
> of mathematic
> circularity

she circumvents the near-impossibility of translating so exotically
natural an impression by pinning down, first of all, the mixture
of hue and likening it to something definite but unexpected —
yes, and not wine but dregs-of-wine — and next by comparing its
form to the at first concrete *pyramids* and then abstract *circularity*.
But the eye that can see "boats/at sea progress white and rigid as
if in a groove" has long since found the secret way of getting at the
truth of the pure first shock of visual impression. Is it a "science of
the eye" or the free daring of imagination that brings opposites
together that had never met before?

Held up to inspection with the same bold fidelity are her animals who, if they are frequently parts of a web of allusions that
ally them to more philosophies than they could dream of, are
always known first and last to us by their beautiful *thisness* of
claws, dapples, quills, delineated with the vital accuracy of a Bew-
ick, the English engraver who cared just as much for the originality of the particulars. We see them not only in their fine suits of
fur and feather, we see them also in the fitness and niceness of
those "skills" by which they earn their livings, defend themselves,
and keep up their populations. We see them as craftsmen and we
see them as artists, too. The frigate pelican hides (as "impassioned
Handel") "in the height and in the majestic/display of his art,"

the jerboa's leaps "should be set/to the flageolet," the "wasp-nest flaws" on the paper nautilus are compared to "the lines in the mane of a Parthenon horse." And sometimes they are compared to works of art or artists. The pangolin, "Leonardo's indubitable son" (in the *What Are Years* version), is "compact like the furled/fringed frill/on the hat brim of Gargallo's hollow iron head of a/matador."

Gide in *Travels in the Congo* wrote of his rare tamed antelope: "I must study Dindiki's ethics and aesthetics, his peculiar manner of moving and defending and protecting himself. Every animal has succeeded in finding out his own particular manner, outside of which there seems to be no salvation for him." It is the beast's particular manner that Marianne Moore has found. The style of the poet — style, "that specialisation of sensibility" — has met the "style" of the animal. Her celebrated objectivity exemplifies that detachment that the West Wind symbolizes in "Half Deity." If it is his delighted disinterest that spurs the butterfly into really becoming a half deity, that same detachment in the artist permits the object, the beast, to be seen for itself, brought into existence or a second existence. Cezanne said: "The landscape is reflected in me and I am its consciousness." When the plumet basilisk is in danger and all his forces leap into play, when he is that "nervous naked sword on little feet," when he has the black eyes of a "molested bird" "with look of whetted fierceness/in what is merely/breathing and recoiling from the hand," we can only feel that the poet has entered into the blood and breath of the beast, transmitting its very reality into our hands, and that observation has become a passion.

Thus her "studies" are always dramas. Each animal poem begins at the point of an action. It's night and the pangolin is setting forth or the frigate pelican has just robbed another bird of its fish, all in mid-air. We have no stuffed animals. She does not, as Audubon did, paint her birds when they're dead. But she is no "externalist." "The power of the visible/is the invisible." Thus the jerboa of the "Chippendale" claws, described as if some Supreme Cabinetmaker had thought him up, is no "conqueror"; he is "free-born," "has happiness" in the abundance of all that he needs which is almost nothing, not even water, and becomes the occasion for a secret discussion on the powers of a being to live in an energy of delight, in spontaneous accord with his portion of the universe. And in "The Pangolin" three refrains of Shakespearean munificence and hymn-like sobriety work against the descriptive weave. As in "The Frigate Pelican" there is the sudden outbreak of the personal voice — *"Festina lente.* Be gay/civilly? How so?" — in the midst of this impersonal improvisation on a bird's flight, so this personal-impersonal refrain is set against the pangolin's "exhausting trips" until at the close, our cousinship with this " 'Fearful yet to be feared' " animal so insinuatingly established (as it was in "Peter" who is "one of those who do not regard/the published fact as a surrender"), we see ourselves and him in a universal context:

> The prey of fear, he, always
> curtailed, extinguished, thwarted by the dusk,
> work partly done,
> says to the alternating blaze,
> 'Again the sun!
> anew each day; and new and new and new,
> that comes into and steadies my soul.'

Danger is three-fourths of an animal's life and its every element; these poems don't let us forget it. For the plumet basilisk it is only nightfall that protects him from men who can kill him. The ostrich has circumvented extinction by his solicitude for his young; the butterfly is pursued by a child, the young birds by a cat; the devilfish must zealously guard her eggs. What thorns of a rose are "proof" against "the predatory hand"? "All are/naked, none is safe." And if "Hercules, bitten/by a crab loyal to the hydra,/was hindered to succeed," there are those who "have lived and lived on every kind of shortage," not unlike the jerboa.

We come into the themes of armor and unarmedness and self-protectiveness, to humility "His shield," to the pangolin again, the "frictionless creep of a thing/made graceful by adversities, con/versities," to the not aggressive, tentative snail whose "contractility" of horns "is a virtue as modesty is a virtue." In "The Fish" the "defiant edifice" with "marks of abuse" upon it "has proved that it can live/on what can not revive/its youth. The sea grows old in it." And one can add "resistance with bent head, like foxtail/millet's" and "tough-grained animals as have . . . earned that fruit of their ability to endure blows," or "that which it is impossible to force, it is impossible to hinder" (as true of poetry as of this vital vegetable, the carrot, of "Radical") and see how many times difficulty, deprivation, "society's not knowing," struggle (even for a strawberry) are themes implied in the early work, more openly stated in the later. In "The Monkey Puzzle" the solitude of singularity is accepted, to be endured, but in "Sojourn in a Whale" it is suggested that the impossible, the constricting condition can be circumvented by the power of the being to "rise on itself" as water does "when obstacles happened to bar/the path" (which is one answer to the complacency of the proverb "Water seeks its own level").

As the themes of the scarred but defiant and enduring interact with the theme of the wild animal's precarious existence, so the themes of bondage and freedom interact with these. "What Are Years?" — that exultant psalm — is built upon the paradox that only in the acceptance of limitations can one be released from them (as the caged bird, "grown taller as he sings, steels/his form straight up" and in "his mighty singing/says, satisfaction is a lowly/thing, how pure a thing is joy"). This Christian paradox is not abandoned. In "His Shield" freedom is defined as "the power of relinquishing/what one would keep"; in "Spenser's Ireland" a reversal: "you're not free/until you've been made captive by/ supreme belief." The devilfish's "intensively/watched eggs coming from/the shell free it when they are freed" suggests not only the gestation of a work but much else. The poem frees the poet when he has expressed it and delivered it. The devilfish who possesses her eggs is as much possessed by them; so is the jailor by the jailed. The freedom of the one is the freedom of the other. In "The Jerboa" the people "who liked little things" but had slaves, kept "power over the poor," and even put baboons to work for them are in bondage compared with the jerboa, both indubitably himself, a happy animal, and emblem of the spirit; they are in bondage to their materialities, their petty customs, rituals, superstitions. The jerboa with nothing but immaterial abundance is free.

So is the elephant of "Melancthon" (formerly "Black Earth"), that earliest of heroes (1918), who has richly accepted the rough conditions of existence, who has survived earthquakes and lightning. He does what he does which pleases no one but himself, his spiritual poise is not in pride (though he is too confident to be humble) but in that kind of seeing and hearing which the senses only have when the soul is master. He trumpets: "My ears are sensitized to more than the sound of/the wind." He is the hardy master of the ("patina of") circumstance like any Chinese sage. Lesser heroes are the cat of "Silence" and "Peter" himself, both eminently self-reliant and honorably what they are, with no apologies.

Other heroes are the student of "The Student" who can "hold by himself" and the hero of "The Hero" who is a kind of hero-in-reverse, without the heroics. Of touchy nerves he doesn't like "suffering and not/saying so." He can also be vexing or, like "Pilgrim having to go slow/to find his roll; tired but hopeful." He is certainly the opposite of the tragic hero or the standard nerveless hero. But, jumpy like the pangolin, he is not empty: he knows "the rock crystal thing to see — the startling El Greco/brimming with inner light — that covets nothing that it has let go."

A facet of the hero is the "decorous frock-coated Negro" "with a/sense of human dignity/and reverence for mystery, standing like the shadow/of the willow." The willow, most pliant of trees and fragile of bough. Heroism, like any good thing, is precariously maintained. (It is also "exhausting.") The seemingly random course of this poem rather beautifully fits the exposition of a hero full of inner hesitations and if it could be said that this poem is a poem about a person who has found his spiritual rock to abide by, it could also be said of "The Steeple-Jack" that it presents us with a vision of the place where this rock might be. Certainly this poem remains one of Miss Moore's most charmed ones. That "Dürer would have seen a reason for living/in a town like this, with eight stranded whales/to look at; with the sweet sea air coming into your house/on a fine day" is already more than enough to establish the tone from which nothing thereafter, not one accent, departs, the tone of a state of what seems to amount to purest felicity. As well, it expresses so fine an appreciation for the irregular, the not self-conscious, the moderate, modest, and free, the slightly crooked, the not-correct but vital, that it remains a triumph of the unexpected, of things caught in their essential dress, their *quidditas*. Nowhere does Miss Moore's zest for the idiosyncratic and genius for selecting the exactly right and irresistible detail shine forth more warmly, from "the whirlwind fife-and-drum of the storm" to the action that keeps danger and hope in tension when the steeple-jack lets down his rope "as a spider spins a thread." There is in this local setting endeared the gusto of a very idiomatic, very home-grown paradise, the only paradise that some of us can believe in, the one that's found, when it is found, on earth, when "there is nothing that ambition can buy or take away."

And in another mode "A Carriage from Sweden" creates out of the view of a "museum-piece . . . country cart/that inner happiness made art" some platonic ideal of "stalwartness, skill" and fey grace. The musical "Spenser's Ireland" creates all the wayward elusiveness of an enchanter's place. Remarkable for its "flax for damask" passage, its "guillemot/so neat and the hen/of the heath," it is the presence of the unsaid far underneath the said that produces at least a half of this delicate combination of magic and ruefulness.

Returning to the subject of the hero, are there not-heroes? Very few. Even her animals are "good," as Randall Jarrell has pointed out. But in "The Hero" there is a "sightseeing hobo," a fool of shameless questions. Very little time is spent on her, no more than is spent on that group of people in "The Icosasphere" who are "avid for someone's fortune." "Through lack of integration" — could understatement be more excessive? — "three were slain and ten committed perjury,/six died, two killed themselves, and" — studied anticlimax — "two paid fines for risks they'd run." For why flay a dead horse? "Heroes need not write an ordinall of attributes to enumer/ate/what they hate." If presidents punish "sin-driven senators by not thinking about them," Miss Moore, it might be inferred, prefers too to ignore certain obvious forms of tawdry or berserk behavior. However that may be, this Websterian plot of misconduct (lacking only incest) is mentioned only in passing and is simply one element in a poem that sets up very dryly relationships between the "rare efficiency" of birds' nests made in "parabolic concentric curves" and the icosasphere that an engineer, lacking the instinct of the birds, had to take infinite pains to learn how to make, and the still living enigma of how the Egyptians ever got their obelisks up. That the birds' nests put mortal "lack

of integration" to shame, and the obelisks Mr. J. O. Jackson's icosasphere, it is left up to the reader to "make out."

Interacting veins between early work and later work are evident
not only in themes but in certain imagery. The elephant, for example, has two whole poems to himself but his trunk turns up in
at least four other poems. The sea appears both early and late,
and so does water imagery. In "The Fish" there is the vividness
of all that scuttling under water life of volatile flux and flow (and
the mysterious correspondence of the "crow-blue" mussel-shell
"opening and shutting itself like/an/injured fan" with the
hatchet-scarred cliff). There is "A Grave," that masterpiece that
calls the sea "a collector, quick to return a rapacious look"
haunted by the beauty of the metaphor that wins life from death:

> men lower nets, unconscious of the fact that they are
>   desecrating a grave,
> and row quickly away — the blades of the oars
> moving together like the feet of water-spiders as if
>   there were no such thing as death.

In "An Egyptian Pulled Glass Bottle in the Shape of a Fish"
there is "a wave held up for us to see/In its essential perpendicu-
larity" while water in "The Steeple-Jack" is "etched with waves
as formal as the scales/on a fish." In "Dock Rats" there is the
"steam yacht, lying/like a new made arrow on the/stream" and
the sea's "horse strength." Not to forget the concluding lines on
the grandeur of the waters in "Novices."

In "Marriage" the image of " 'the heart rising/in its estate of
peace/as a boat rises/with the rising of the water' " suggests not
only the image of water in "Sojourn in a Whale" but the central
image in "What Are Years?" of the one who "in his imprisonment
rises/upon himself as/the sea in a chasm, struggling to be/free."

The birds of "A Grave" that "swim through the air at top
speed" remind one of the seagulls in "The Steeple-Jack" "flying

back and forth over the town clock" and the beautiful merry-go-round study of the frigate pelican's flight. In "In the Days of Prismatic Colour" we might associate the cliff of "The Fish" with what survives, what is organic to existence, the very bedrock of things as it is celebrated in the lines

> Truth is no Apollo
> Belvedere, no formal thing. The wave may go over it if
> it likes.
> Know that it will be there when it says,
> 'I shall be there when the wave has gone by.'

But though certain themes and imagery appear and reappear, there is a continuous unfolding, a deepening and widening of range, a constant experimenting with new modes or new aspects of a form. "Half Deity," notable for its symmetrical beauty, is a little model of dramatic development, the West Wind acting as a *deus ex machina* to allow for the butterfly's full emergence, full achievement of his transfiguration. ("Bird-Witted" is another, less formally elaborated.) "In Distrust of Merits," written during World War II, achieves, with its powerful rhythmic impulsion, its refrain, "They're fighting, fighting, fighting," majestic scope and harrowing depth. But it is particularly by the veracity of the poet's own directly subjective voice questioning, self-questioning, holding dialogue with itself, that the poem achieves its moral power. "They're fighting that I/may yet recover from the disease, My/Self; some have it lightly; some will die. 'Man/wolf to man' and we devour/ourselves." It is in such ways that Miss Moore's "morals" become a way of seeing the eternal. Again the theme of heroic acceptance that is also withstanding, that may become transcendence, is exemplified in the lines " 'When a man is prey to anger,/he is moved by outside things; when he holds/his ground in patience patience/patience, that is action or/beauty.' " (And "Beauty is everlasting/and dust is for a time" the poem concludes.)

We see again her democratic hero's aristocratic self-sufficiency based upon his endeavor at self-knowledge, the aesthetic of his ethics. Indeed, Miss Moore's awareness of the incessant conflict that the "firebrand that is life" is grounded in gives her poetry that gusto of what she has called "helpless" sincerity.

It is an aside to point out that at least two of her animals, the impalla and the tuatera, will soon become extinct unless they are put on a list of animals-to-be-preserved-in-zoos, though it is an aside pertinent to other rareties always in danger of becoming extinct. Against such general pervasive threat her various later poems, "Efforts of Affection," "Voracities and Verities," "By Disposition of Angels," yield us searching insights to "steady the soul," ending on "Bach-cheerful" tonic chords of affirmation. One all but hears the lofty resoluteness of Lutheran hymns.

But how awkward it is to paraphrase. It goes against the tight grain of these poems to expatiate upon their themes, for they are never as openly stated as this kind of generalizing might lead some innocent reader to suppose. Rather, insights always seem pulled from out the very heart of the particulars:

> What is there
> like fortitude! What sap
> went through that little thread
> to make the cherry red!

This comes in "Nevertheless" as if it had been a secret wrenched forth just at that moment when happening upon the trials of a plant she saw how in its *élan vital* it had persisted. And thus her moral insights seem "proved on the pulse" to use Keats's phrase; they taste of the savor of conflict, they are the secret truths fought for and not the hawked wise-saws, the maxims of the copybooks.

Marianne Moore is, as she said of William Carlos Williams, "indomitably American," whether she is with sweet reasonableness correcting its critics (in "England") or joking upon "the original American menagerie of styles" (in "An Octopus"), although the earlier debate between past and present, Europe and America, is far less noticeable in her later work. Like Emily Dickinson she is irresistibly original. With Thoreau she dislikes the showy ("I don't like diamonds"), which includes gardenia scent and the overemphatic, all of which is at one with her capacity to make us feel the finest shadings.

By the patience and passion of her "eye" she has proved that the stripes of the tulip *can be counted*; her greater glasses, one might say, have revealed to us how much had not been seen until she saw. By her excitable "detecting" (a numinous word for her) she has given us a new world of marvelous specifics or a new-old world of what had been seen before but seen without feeling. This is to say it had not been seen at all.

The god of irony, the god of humor ("Humor saves a few steps, it saves years"), the god of all-powerful detail (as Pasternak had said) attend her, to preserve her lines in the salt of their rich indigenous honesties.

⤳ Selected Bibliography

Works of Marianne Moore

POETRY

Poems. London: Egoist Press, 1921.
Marriage. New York: Manikin, Number Three, Monroe Wheeler, 1923.
Observations. New York: Dial Press, 1924.
Selected Poems. New York: Macmillan; London: Faber and Faber, 1935. (With an Introduction by T. S. Eliot.)
The Pangolin and Other Verse. London: Brendin Publishing Company, 1936.
What Are Years. New York: Macmillan, 1941.
Nevertheless. New York: Macmillan, 1944.
A Face. Cummington, Mass.: Cummington Press, 1949.
Collected Poems. New York: Macmillan; London: Faber and Faber, 1951.
The Fables of La Fontaine. New York: Viking, 1954. *Selected Fables of La Fontaine*. London: Faber and Faber, 1955. (Translation.)
Like a Bulwark. New York: Viking, 1956.
O to Be a Dragon. New York: Viking, 1959.

PROSE

Predilections. New York: Viking, 1955; London: Faber and Faber, 1956. (Essays.)
The Ford correspondence. *New Yorker*, 33:140–46 (April 13, 1957). Reprinted by Pierpont Morgan Library, New York, 1958.
Puss in Boots, The Sleeping Beauty, and Cinderella, by Charles Perrault, adapted by Marianne Moore. New York: Macmillan, 1963.

READER

A Marianne Moore Reader. New York: Viking, 1961.

CURRENT AMERICAN REPRINT

A Marianne Moore Reader. New York: Compass (Viking Press). $1.65.

Bibliography

Sheehy, Eugene P., and Kenneth A. Lohf. *The Achievement of Marianne Moore: A Bibliography 1907–1957*. New York: New York Public Library, 1958.

Critical and Biographical Studies

Blackmur, R. P. "The Method of Marianne Moore," in *Language as Gesture*. New York: Harcourt, Brace, 1952.

Burke, Kenneth. "Motives and Motifs in the Poetry of Marianne Moore," *Accent*, 2:157–69 (Spring 1942).

———. "Likings of an Observationist," *Poetry*, 87:239–47 (January 1956).

Doolittle, Hilda (H. D.). "Marianne Moore," *Egoist*, 3 (no. 8):118–19 (August 1916).

Eliot, T. S. A review of *Marriage* and *Poems*, in *Dial*, 75:594–97 (December 1923).

Frankenberg, Lloyd. "The Imaginary Garden," in *Pleasure Dome*. Boston: Houghton Mifflin, 1949. Pp. 119–50.

Gregory, Horace, and Marya Zaturenska. "Marianne Moore: The Genius of *The Dial*," in *The History of American Poetry, 1900–1940*. New York: Harcourt, Brace, 1946. Pp. 317–25.

Hall, Donald. Interview, *Paris Review*, 7:41–66 (Winter 1961).

Hoffman, Frederick J. *The Twenties: American Writing in the Postwar Decade*. New York: Viking, 1955. Pp. 176–79, 260–61, and *passim*.

Jarrell, Randall. *Poetry and the Age*. New York: Knopf, 1953.

"Marianne Moore Issue," *Quarterly Review of Literature*, 4 (no. 2):121–223 (1948), edited by José Garcia Villa. (Contains essays by Elizabeth Bishop, Louise Bogan, Cleanth Brooks, George Dillon, Wallace Fowlie, Lloyd Frankenberg, Vivienne Koch, John Crowe Ransom, Wallace Stevens, John L. Sweeney, William Carlos Williams, T. C. Wilson.)

Pound, Ezra. "Marianne Moore and Mina Loy," *Little Review*, 4:57–58 (March 1918). Reprinted in *The Little Review Anthology*, edited by Margaret Anderson. New York: Hermitage House, 1953. Pp. 188–89.

Tate, Allen. *Sixty American Poets, 1896–1944*. Washington, D.C.: U.S. Library of Congress, 1954.

Williams, William Carlos. "Marianne Moore," *Dial*, 78:393–401 (May 1925).

Winters, Yvor. "Holiday and Day of Wrath," *Poetry*, 26:39–44 (April 1925).

———. *In Defense of Reason*. New York: Swallow Press and W. Morrow, 1947.

Zabel, Morton Dauwen. "A Literalist of the Imagination," *Poetry*, 47:326–36 (March 1936).